Johnny Depp

Julia Holt

Published in association with The Basic Skills Agency

Hodder & Stoughton

A MEMBER OF THE HODDER HEADLINE GROUP

HIGH SCHOOL

Acknowledgements
Cover: Ed Geller/Retna
Photos: p 3 Armando Gallo/Retna; p 6 Marion Samuels/Retna; p 10 Topham Picturepoint;
p 13 The Ronald Grant Archive; p 17 Alpha; p 19 Doug Peters/All Action, p 24 PA Photos;
p26 Sam Levi/Retna Ltd.

Every effort has been made to trace copyright holders of material reproduced in this book.
Any rights not acknowledged will be acknowledged in subsequent printings if notice is
given to the publisher.

Orders; please contact Bookpoint Ltd, 39 Milton Park, Abingdon, Oxon OX14 4TD.
Telephone (44) 01235 400414, Fax: (44) 01235 400454. Lines are open from 9.00–6.00,
Monday to Saturday, with a 24 hour message answering service.
Email address: orders@bookpoint.co.uk

British Library Cataloguing in Publication Data
A catalogue record for this title is available from The British Library

ISBN 0 340 80099 2

First published 2001
Impression number   10 9 8 7 6 5 4 3 2 1
Year   2007 2006 2005 2004 2003 2002 2001

Copyright © 2001 Julia Holt

Typeset by SX Composing DTP, Rayleigh, Essex
Printed in Great Britain for Hodder & Stoughton Educational, a division of Hodder Headline
Plc, 338 Euston Road, London NW1 3BH by Redwood Books, Trowbridge, Wiltshire

Contents

1 John Depp III

Johnny Depp says
he is not 'Mr Blockbuster.'
He likes to make different films.
He is different
from other teenage heart-throbs.
He has grown up
to be respected as a good actor.
He has done this
by making unusual films.

Johnny was born on 9 June 1963
in Kentucky.
He was a small-town boy.
He was the fourth child in the family.
His parents named him John Depp III
after his father and grandfather.

Johnny spent
the first seven years of his life
with his grandfather.
His grandfather was a Cherokee Indian.
The two of them
picked tobacco together.
They were very close.

When his grandfather died
the family moved
down the coast to Miami.
They kept moving house.
Sometimes they lived in motels.
As Johnny grew up
the family moved over twenty times.
He didn't bother making friends
because he knew they would move on.

Johnny Depp.

Johnny found it hard to fit in at school.
He was an unusual child.
He was keen on music
and World War II.
He dug tunnels in the back yard
like the soldiers in Vietnam.
Then he went into the tunnel
and waited for it to fall in on him.

When he was twelve,
Johnny's mum got him
an electric guitar.
He shut himself in his room
and learned to play.

Johnny hated school.
He was very bored.
He got in with a bad crowd
and started stealing and taking drugs.
But all that stopped
when he was fifteen.

His parents split up.
Johnny's mum needed a lot of help
to sort herself out.
Johnny helped her.
He had his mum's name
tattooed on his arm
inside a red heart.
Later he had an Indian Chief's head
tattooed on the other arm.

Johnny dropped out of school
to play in his band.
They were called The Kids.
They played in all the clubs
up and down Florida.
He made $24 a week.
When he was twenty
he married one of his fans.
She was called Lori.
Together they tried to get
a record deal for the band
with no success.
After two years
Johnny and Lori split up.

Johnny performing with The Kids.

2 Johnny goes to Hollywood

Johnny and his band
went to Hollywood to find work.
They didn't make much money
so Johnny got a job
selling pens over the phone.
He hated the job
and tried to get work in films.

His first acting job
was in *Nightmare on Elm Street*.
He played a boy
who gets killed by Freddy Kruger.
Johnny had never had so much money
in all his life.
Over the next two years
he took acting lessons.
The band broke up
and Johnny got small acting jobs.

In 1986 Johnny was sent
the script for the film *Platoon*.
He was given a part in the film
and was told they would be filming
in the jungle.
Platoon was a Vietnam War story.

For the first thirteen days
all the actors went into training.
They were trained like real soldiers.
They did sixty-mile treks
in the jungle.
It was very hard work.
Platoon was a big success
and the critics liked Johnny's work.

Next Johnny was wanted
for TV work.
He didn't really want to do it.
He signed up
to make one series
of *21 Jump Street*.
It was about undercover cops
looking for drugs in schools.

The series was made
in Vancouver.
In 1987 Johnny moved there.
He took his mum
and her new husband with him.
The series was a big, big hit
with teenagers.
Johnny got 10,000 fan letters a month.
He was on the front of teen magazines
every week.

Starring in *21 Jump Street* turned Johnny into a heart-throb.

Being on *21 Jump Street*
gave Johnny time
to learn about acting.
But he didn't want
to be a heart-throb.
He was very glad
when he left the series.

In 1989 Johnny met Winona Ryder.
They met six months
before they made
Edward Scissorhands together.
Before long Johnny and Winona
were engaged and living together.
They became the top Hollywood couple.
Johnny had 'Winona Forever'
tattooed on his arm.

In *Edward Scissorhands*
Johnny played a man-made boy
who lives alone.
Edward has scissors for hands.
He is later adopted by the Avon lady
and her family.
At first he is popular
but then he is bullied
and chased away.

The film was a big success.
It made Johnny a star
all over the world.

Edward Scissorhands was a huge success.

3   Hollywood Bad Boy

The press followed Johnny
and Winona everywhere.
He didn't like it and told them so.
He became the latest
Hollywood bad boy.

For the next two years
Johnny and Winona
were gossiped about in every paper.
But their work kept them apart
and in 1993 they split up.
Johnny had his tattoo changed
to 'Wino Forever'.

Johnny was very upset.
He said: 'It's very hard
to have a personal life in Hollywood.'

In 1993, Johnny played another odd ball
in *Benny and Joon*.
It is a love story about
two misfits.
He had to learn a lot of magic tricks
for the film.
Johnny said:
'I'm attracted to these off-beat parts
because my life has been
a bit abnormal.'

Johnny's next film, *What's Eating Gilbert Grape*,
was a bit like his own life.
He played a boy
who looks after his mum
and his brother.
In the film, Leonardo DiCaprio
plays his brother.
Johnny and Leo
were very good together.

But Johnny was missing Winona.
He was drinking
and smoking too much.
Then on the night of Hallowe'en 1993
things started to go
very wrong for Johnny.
He owned a club called The Viper Room.
That night, a young star
called River Phoenix
died of a drug overdose
outside the club.

One paper called The Viper Room
'Depp's Den of Sex, Drugs and Death.'
It was a big scandal.

River Phoenix died of an overdose outside The Viper Room.

In February 1994
Johnny met Kate Moss.
She was a supermodel
and eleven years younger than Johnny.
Again the press
followed them everywhere.

Seven months later
Johnny was in jail
for trashing a hotel room.
He was still the bad boy of Hollywood.

In October 1995
Johnny bought a house
in Hollywood.
Not just any old house.
It cost $2.3 million.
It used to be the home
of Bela Lugosi.
He used to play Dracula
in the old black and white films.
People call it the castle
because it looks like
Dracula's castle.

Johnny and Kate Moss.

In the same year
Johnny made a bid
to get away from
his misfit films.
He made a thriller.
It was called *Nick of Time*.

Johnny played a man
whose little girl is kidnapped.
To get her back
he has to kill someone.
He has ninety minutes to do it.
He has to race against the clock.
The film asks:
'What would you do
if you were him?'

Johnny and Kate split up in 1997.
She said they had too many fights.
He said she was too moody.

In the same year,
Johnny was in a gangster film.
It was called *Donnie Brasco*.
He played a Mafia informer.
He was very good in this film.

Then he went back
to playing off-beat people again.
He had a part in *Fear and Loathing in Las Vegas*.
It is the story of a reporter,
his writing and his drug taking.
The film wasn't a big success
because it was
difficult to understand.

4 Paris

Johnny was in Paris
in the summer of 1998.
He was filming *The Ninth Gate*.
It is a horror film.

In the middle of filming
he met Vanessa Paradis.
She is a singer and an actress.
After a few months
they were living together in Paris
and Vanessa was pregnant.
Their daughter, Lily-Rose, was born
on 27 May 1999.

In the months
before Lily-Rose was born
Johnny went to England
to make the film *Sleepy Hollow*.
It is a classic story
set in 1799.

In the small village of Sleepy Hollow
some men have been murdered.
The villagers send for a policeman,
played by Johnny Depp.
The villagers think the murders
have been done
by a headless horseman.
Johnny thinks otherwise.
He has to go
into a scary forest
to catch the murderer.

Johnny Depp with director Tim Burton and co-stars Christina Ricci and Casper Van Dien.

Back home in Paris
life is very different for Johnny.
He can go out in the city
and not be followed.
He feels at home there
with his new family.
He is learning French
to keep up with Lily-Rose.

Johnny has four films
in the pipeline
and they are all very different.
The Man Who Cried
is a story about World War II.
Chocolat is about
a chocolate shop in France.
In the film *Blow* Johnny plays
a South American drug smuggler.
Later on Johnny will play a policeman
who is trying to catch Jack the Ripper
in the film *From Hell*.

Johnny Depp and Vanessa Paradis.

Johnny took a big risk
working on all those
unusual films.
But it paid off.
People remember his films.

Johnny has settled down in France.
He and Vanessa
want to have more children.
This seems to have saved him.
He says that he works for Hollywood
but he doesn't have to live there.